UNLOCKING
SPIRITUAL
AUTHORITY

by Jonas Clark

Unless otherwise noted, Scripture quotations are taken from the King James Version.

UNLOCKING SPIRITUAL AUTHORITY

ISBN-10: 1-886885-42-7

ISBN-13: 978-1-886885-42-4

Published by Jonas Clark Ministries

27 West Hallandale Beach Blvd.

Hallandale, Florida, 33009-5437, U.S.A.

(954) 456-4420

www.JonasClark.com

Printed in India

UNLOCKING SPIRITUAL AUTHORITY

Your kingship was God's Orginal intention and He hasn't changed His mind. From the moment Adam lost his kingship (spiritual authority) and was expelled from the Garden of Eden God has been working all things after the counsel of His will—to restore this world and everything in it back to Himself.

Luke records God's plan in Acts 3:19-21:

"Repent ye therefore, and be converted, that your sins may be blotted out, when the times of refreshing shall come from the presence of the Lord; And he shall send Jesus Christ, which before was preached unto you: Who the heaven must receive until the times of restitution of all things, which God hath spoken by the mouth of all his holy prophets since the world began."

RESTORING WHAT WAS LOST

Restoration is the act of restoring to the rightful owner something that has been taken away, lost or stolen. The word "restitution" in this Scripture comes from the Greek word apokatastasis, meaning "to return this earth back to its perfect state before the fall." God has been working to restore the earth to its perfect state and to restore man's kingship for thousands of years.

In the beginning, we know that God created Adam in His own image, in His likeness and with His nature (Genesis 1:26). The Word says that "God formed man from the dust of the ground and breathed life (not air) into his nostrils and man became a living soul with purpose—to fellowship with God and have dominion over this earth (Genesis 2:7; 1:26).

In the original creation Adam was perfect. He lived out of his spirit. He communed with God out of his spirit. He was connected to God through his spirit. He named the animals from his spirit. He tended the garden from his spirit. He exercised his kingship, or dominion, over the earth from his spirit.

We were designed from the beginning to take dominion over this earth that God has created. We can never see our original intent restored until we are first born again and subsequently learn to live out of our born-again spirits.

Scripture tells us that God put Adam in the Garden of Eden to dress it and to keep it. He also gave Adam a command:

> "Of every tree of the garden thou mayest freely eat: But of the tree of the knowledge of good and evil, thou shalt not eat of it: for in the day that thou eatest thereof thou shalt surely die" (Genesis 2).

Of course, Adam did not immediately die when he ate of the fruit. He lived to be 930 years old. God was talking about a spiritual death.

Some time after this we read the testimony of Eve's deception by the serpent. That old serpent told Eve that the reason God didn't want her to eat of the tree of the knowledge of good and evil was because her eyes would be opened and she would be like God (Genesis 3:5). The reality was that Adam and Eve were already like God. They were created with the very nature of God, in the image of God, blessed by God, and given dominion over the earth by God.

We all know the sad conclusion, Eve partook and Adam did, too. Sin entered the earth and Adam's spirit died because the wages of sin is death (Romans 6:23). Adam's disobedience caused a communal disconnect between his spirit and the Spirit of God. Adam and Eve began to live out of their souls instead of their spirits. (Your soul is your mind, will, intellect, reasoning, imaginations and emotions.) They were led by their five senses—touch, hearing, sight, smell and taste—instead of their spirits. Before the fall they simply knew what they needed to know. They could draw any knowledge they needed directly from God's Spirit. Their fall was the genesis of soulish education.

When God came into the garden to fellowship with Adam, he heard the Lord's voice and tried to hide among the trees. God called out to Adam, asking "Where art thou?" Adam replied,

> "I heard thy voice in the garden, and I was afraid because I was naked; and I hid myself" (Genesis 2:8-10).

Of course, God knew where Adam was all along. God is all knowing. He didn't ask because He didn't know. God knew where Adam was physically but He couldn't find Adam in His Spirit. For the first time Adam was not connected to God through his spirit.

From that moment on, God determined to restore mankind back to Himself. I can almost hear God saying, "Adam, I'm coming to get you!" In order to work this out to the counsel of His will, God had to send the Second Adam, the Lord Jesus Christ, the Lamb of God that taketh away the sin of the world.

What we need to understand here is that Adam didn't fall from heaven. He fell from grace and rulership. Our ultimate destination as born-again believers is not heaven, but earth. Even the rapture only takes us to heaven for a short time. We will eventually return to this earth to rule and reign with Christ. We don't need incorruptible resurrected bodies to live in heaven. We need them for life on earth.

MANIFESTING SONS

Adam did not understand his purpose. Not understanding our purpose is the foundation of all failure. God's original intent for man has always been to fellowship with Him. We were designed from the beginning to take dominion over this earth that God has created. We can never see our original intent restored until we are first born again and subsequently learn to live out of our born-again spirits.

Scripture says that the Holy Spirit is our Teacher who will lead us and guide us in all truth. He is the One who is actively involved in the restitution of all things. Friend, the Spirit-led life is the answer to walking out your kingship. The Apostle Peter said we are a priesthood of kings (1 Peter 2:9). Jesus said it is the Father's good pleasure to give us the Kingdom (Luke 12:32). Scripture declares,

> "For the earnest expectation of the creature waiteth for the manifestation of the sons of God. For the creature was made subject to vanity, not willingly, but by reason of him who hath subjected the same in hope, Because the creature itself also shall be delivered from the bondage of corruption into the glorious liberty of the children of God." (Romans 8:19-21).

How can we manifest as sons? By exercising our kingship authority as believers and walking out the restored biblical truths of our generation. Every "movement" throughout history has resulted in some form of truth being restored to the Body of Christ. After the resurrection of Jesus, religious spirits attacked the Church and we plunged into the Dark Ages. Yet the seed of the Kingdom of God had already been planted and was destined to outgrow everything.

> "And he said, Whereunto shall we liken the kingdom of God? or with what comparison shall we compare it? It is like a grain of mustard seed, which, when it is sown in the earth, is less than all the seeds that be in the earth: 32 But when it is sown, it groweth up, and becometh greater than all herbs, and shooteth out great branches; so that the fowls of the air may lodge under the shadow of it" (Mark 4:30-32).

We, the believers, are those kings. Jesus has given us authority as priests and kings. We have a solid revelation of our priesthood, but we have yet to fully comprehend what it means to be a royal (kingly) priesthood.

Consider this. It took over 2,000 years for the Church to be prepared for the restoration of this "kingship of every believer" truth. What we do with this revelation of kingship, as the original intent is up to us.

We need to lay hold God's government—and our kingship—before we can see true reform in the Church. Jesus is the King of kings and the Lord of lords. He is the King of Glory Who rules His Church. He is the King of the Universe with servants, ambassadors, armies, enemies, and, yes, a fully functional government.

11

The Prophet Isaiah declared that there would be no end to the increase of His government and peace. Jesus is predestined to reign on David's throne over His Kingdom, establishing and upholding it with judgment and justice forever (Isaiah 9:7).

Most of us are familiar with Isaiah's prophetic decree, but does the Body of Christ truly recognize that the seat of Jesus' rule on earth is in the local church? Or has religion tainted our view of the local church by portraying it as merely a gathering place for believers to worship God and listen to a Sunday morning motivational sermon? In some sad cases the local church has been reduced to nothing more that a social club with a religious montage.

MANIFESTING THE KINGDOM OF GOD

The restoration of apostles is shedding new light on the local church as not only a gathering place for believers to get equipped to do the work of the ministry but also as a governmental center in a spiritual jurisdiction assigned by God. Local church leaders and believers, then, must understand the government of God in order to be most effective in accomplishing its mandate to manifest the Kingdom of God.

Looking at the structure and function of natural governments can help us to better understand spiritual governments. While natural governments include senators, ambassadors and presidents, for example, spiritual governments include apostles, prophets, evangelists, pastors, teachers, priests and kings. Scripture declares,

"And God hath set some in the church, first apostles, secondarily prophets, thirdly teachers, after that miracles, then gifts of healings, helps, governments, diversities of tongues" (1 Corinthians 12:28).

In both realms, governing is ruling by right of authority, administering policy, exercising power, and regulating, influencing, restraining and managing the affairs of men.

So if Jesus is the King of kings and Lord of lords, and He is, then just who are these kings that Jesus is King of? We, the believers, are those kings. Jesus has given us authority as priests and kings. We have a solid revelation of our priesthood—we can sing, worship, preach, pray and prophesy with the best of them; we can cast out demons and lay hands on the sick and watch them recover—but we have yet to fully comprehend what it means to be a royal (kingly) priesthood.

SPIRITUAL JURISDICTIONS

God sets churches in territories as governmental centers filled with believers who are called to invade, occupy, influence and manifest the dominion of the Kingdom of God on earth just as it is in heaven. As kings who have been planted and sent out from local churches we have been assigned places of spiritual jurisdictions (domains) in which to rule and reign and to establish heaven's rule on earth.

How will we see His Kingdom come on earth as it is in heaven? Demonstrating kingship through evangelism is the key to changing cities because when people are saved and baptized in the Holy Ghost the devil will lose his grip on the crime-riddled, drug infested neighborhoods he set out to destroy. As we reach out to the lost, we build the Church of Jesus Christ and establish His Kingdom in our territories.

BUILDING GRACE

Jesus, our High Priest, King, Lord and Chief Apostle, has assured us that He is building His Church and the gates of hell will not prevail against it (Matthew 16:18). Take note that Jesus is not building His Church in heaven and no demon power is opposing His heavenly government. No, Jesus is building His Church and establishing His Kingdom here, and we— as priests and kings with an apostolic building grace— are called to help Him. You might say our Lord is the Lead Architect and we are the construction workers that follow His blueprint to build His Church.

The Author and Finisher of our faith is also a Warrior and He is using us as a battleaxe to overcome demonic enemies opposing His rule on earth. The battle against Jesus' governing rulership is directed against every believer and the local church in particular. The gates of hell have shut down many a local church and caused many other once-on-fire believers to hang up their armor and head for the hills. The apostolic grace imparted to believers equips them to break through the spiritual resistance to building the Church and living a strong Christian life.

INVADING DARK KINGDOMS

The Apostle Paul equipped the believers at Ephesus with spiritual weapons to victoriously battle the forces raging against the government of God on earth. The wise masterbuilder said,

Jesus gave His Church the right to exercise His majestic authority, challenge anything that opposes His Word, resist demon principalities and powers, decree a thing, announce, command, influence, and, yes, govern.

"We wrestle not against flesh and blood, but against principalities, against powers, against the rulers of the darkness of this world, against spiritual wickedness in high places" (Ephesians 6:12).

The Greek word for "principalities" is *arche*, meaning the habitation of demonic government. He then proceeded to equip them by imparting faith, truth, the Word of God, revelations of their righteousness in

Christ, their salvation and the importance of invading the kingdoms of darkness by spreading the Gospel.

Paul's strong words in his epistle to the Ephesians capture the essence of the fight to stop the local church from equipping believers to rule and reign as priests and kings. It paints a vivid picture of the wiles of the enemy designed to hinder believers from governing spiritually and influencing naturally. The devil knows that the local church connects the spiritual realm with the natural realm. The evil one understands that the local church is more than the house of God; it is also the gate of heaven. Remember Jacob's ladder? The Bible records Jacob's powerful dream in which he saw the Lord atop a ladder that stretched from the earth below into the heavens above. Jacob saw angelic beings ascending and descending on that ladder delivering divine assignments directly to the servants of God. He called the footrest of that ladder the house of God, the gate of heaven (Genesis 28:10-17).

As Christ's ambassadors, we need to understand that Jacob's prophetic dream portrays local churches today. The local church is a house of prayer, where revelation, strategies, instruction, direction, warning and the prophetic voice are released into the heart of God's victorious believers. It is where the Holy Spirit governs through His Word, His voice and His people. It is the place for the perfecting of saints and the gathering of sent ones and companies, all called to take the Kingdom of God into the heart of their cities (Acts 13).

Paul also told the Ephesians that it is now God's intent for His Church to make His manifold wisdom known to the rulers and authorities in those same high places (Ephesians 3:10). Making His wisdom known is accomplished through the act of exercising and demonstrating His righteous rule on earth.

AMBASSADORS OF CHRIST

Finally, Paul taught the Corinthians that Jesus must rule through His Church by continuing to put down all opposing spiritual government, authority, and power, thus subduing all His enemies under His feet (1 Corinthians 15:24-28). Jesus gave His Church the right to exercise His majestic authority, challenge anything that opposes His Word, resist demon principalities and powers, decree a thing, announce, command, influence, and, yes, govern.

Jesus has entrusted His government to His Church. We must not lose sight of the truth that local churches are set in territories and have an awesome responsibility to invade and occupy with the Gospel of Jesus Christ. Believers are ambassadors of God's government—ambassadors are the highest-ranking representatives of a government or kingdom—and every believer is called to actively represent and demonstrate the rule of God on earth (2 Corinthians 5:20).

When you understand the governmental function of the local church, then you can find your place in it as a believer. Remember, "You are a chosen generation, a royal priesthood, a holy nation, a peculiar people; that you should show forth the praises of him who hath called you out of darkness into his marvelous light" (1 Peter 2:9). Keep in mind that Jesus said He is building His church—not a ministry that is disconnected from the local church. If you help build what He is building—the local church—then the "increase of His government" will come on you, too.

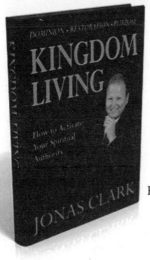

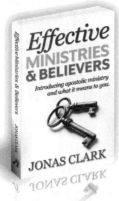

ISBN 1-886885-26-5

WANT MORE?
Read Imaginations, Dare to Win the battle Against your Mind

Are people talking about you behind your back? Do you have confrontational conversations with them in your mind? Does your husband really want to leave you? Or is it just your imagination?

Get equipped to discern the devil's attacks against your mind.

In this book, Jonas teaches you to cast down evil imaginations and tap into prophetic imaginations. You'll discover:

- How to recognize the subtle suggestions of the whisperer.
- How to stop invisible opponents.
- How to overcome the enemies in your mind.
- How to tap into your God-given prophetic imagination.
- How to walk where dreams live.
- And much more...

Order Online at www.JonasClark.com
or call 800.943.6490.

AVOIDING FOREIGN SPIRITS

Foreign spirits are entering churches and ministries undetected. Prophetic people are first targets of these deceiving spirits. Prophesy, for example, is not something done by faith alone. Accuracy requires unction from the Holy Ghost. Faith alone will not force the Holy Spirit to speak. Yes there is a measure of faith involved but the prophet does not make prophetic utterances come by faith. The seasoned prophet understands this and is able to protect himself and others from prophetic error and foreign spirits.

ISBN 1-886885-40-0

Discover these truths...

- Why you need God's permission to prophesy.
- Five steps for receiving prophetic permission.
- Keys to prophetic maturity.
- How to judge prophecy.
- Avoiding seducing spirits of deception.
- And much more...

Order Online at www.JonasClark.com or call 800.943.6490.

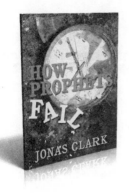

HOW PROPHETS FAIL

Not every prophet makes it.

Power, money, prestige, honor, promotion, and enticements with flattering smooth sayings are all demonic assignments designed to pull on any common ground that might be in the heart of God's prophetic ministers. Understanding high level demonic enticements will protect you from error.

ISBN 1-886885-43-5

Topics include:

- Avoiding the dark side.
- Understanding prophetic enticements.
- Guarding the prophet's heart.
- Steps for emerging prophets.
- Prophets and pitfalls.
- And much more...

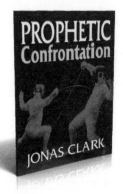

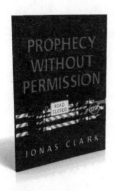

ENTERING PROPHETIC MINISTRY

Prophets carry a great sense of spiritual authority. They enjoy rooting out, pulling down and destroying all spiritual opposition that gets in the way of the plans and purpose of God.

ISBN 1-886885-29-X

In this book discover:

- How prophets see what others cannot.
- Why prophets carry a great sense of spiritual authority.
- Why prophets are the most spiritually sensitive of all the five-fold ministry gifts.
- How prophets steward the mysteries of God.
- How prophets challenge dead traditions of men and dangerous spirits of religion.
- How to enter prophetic ministry.
- Receiving prophetic permission.

MORE EASY READ POCKET-SIZE BOOKS BY JONAS CLARK

Pocket-Size Books

Entering Prophetic Ministry

Prophecy Without Permission

How Witchcraft Spirits Attack

Seeing What Others Can't

Unlocking Prophetic Imaginations

What To Do When You Feel Like Giving Up

The Weapons Of Your Warfare

Overcoming Dark Imaginations

Healing Rejection and Emotional Abuse

Breaking Christian Witchcraft

Prophetic Confrontations

Unlocking Spiritual Authority

Avoiding Foreign Spirits

How Jezebel Hijacks Prophetic Ministry

How Prophets Fail

Identifying Prophetic Spiritists

**Order Online at www.JonasClark.com
or call 800.943.6490.**

Equipping Resources by Jonas Clark

Books

Extreme Prophetic Studies

Advanced Apostolic Studies

Kingdom Living: How to Activate Your Spiritual Authority

Imaginations: Dare to Win the Battle Against Your Mind

Jezebel, Seducing Goddess of War *(Also Available in Spanish)*

Exposing Spiritual Witchraft

30 Pieces of Silver *(Overcoming Religious Spirits)*

The Apostolic Equipping Dimension

Effective Ministries & Believers

Life After Rejection: God's Path to Emotional Healing

Come Out! A Handbook for the Serious Deliverance Minister

Saboteurs in The Republic: Battling Spiritual Wickedness in High Places

Order Online at www.JonasClark.com or call 800.943.6490.